Baseball Hitting Drills for a Batting Tee

Practice Drills for Baseball, Book 1

By Doug Bernier

Baseball Hitting Drills for a Batting Tee: Practice Drills for Baseball, Book 1

Photographs and digital artwork: Sarah Bernier

Additional Photo Credit: Frank Lauri

Cover and book design: Sarah Bernier

ISBN-13: 978-0615747835

ISBN-10: 0615747833

TABLE OF CONTENTS

Important Notice about Free Videos

By purchasing this book, you are now qualified to receive free access to the videos that were created to accompany it – one short video for each drill in the book.

We know that video can be very helpful when communicating how to perform a physical action. In these free videos, author and professional baseball player Doug Bernier demonstrates the proper mechanics for each drill, and briefly describes benefits, correct form, and common mistakes to avoid.

- The code to unlock your free videos is: **BattingTeeDrills**
- Where to enter the code: http://probaseballinsider.com/freevideo1

There is no cost beyond the initial purchase price of the book. In order to receive these videos, simply sign up at http://probaseballinsider.com/freevideo1 to receive email updates about future books and include this code **BattingTeeDrills**. Once you subscribe, you will receive instant access to all 20 videos – one for each drill in this book.

DEDICATION:

This book is dedicated to every person who respects the game of baseball and plays hard.

FOREWARD

Forward by Albie Pearson, former MLB Rookie-of-the-Year & MLB ALL-Star

As I watch the game of baseball evolve, I see the speed of the game and the proficiency of the players growing exponentially. To make it to the highest levels of baseball, players have to be more prepared and work harder than ever before in history. Baseball drills, especially drills off a tee, are a critical part of self-improvement for baseball players. It takes time and many thousands of swings to craft an effective baseball swing, and to make that swing so second-nature that your body will react with good mechanics when you face live pitching and split-second timing in a game.

In my experience, the difference between those who make it in baseball and those who don't is consistency… repeating your swing with drills is an important part of being consistent. Working on a tee is essential to understanding the nuances of your swing so that you can remain consistent, even when you are having an off day at the plate.

This book contains great drills that will help you develop your swing into a tool that can take you to the next level in baseball. Doug has been privileged to play professional baseball with and learn from some of the best hitters in the Major Leagues. He is also a smart player who understands the game of baseball and can break it down in ways that are easy to understand and duplicate. I highly recommend this book of drills as a tool to help yourself, your team, or your child develop into a highly effective hitter.

– **Albie Pearson**, 1958 American League Rookie of the Year, 1963 American League All-star, Former Scout New York Yankees. Currently, Albie and his wife are full-time ministers who, among other projects, founded the Father's Heart Ranch for abused, neglected and abandoned 6 – 12 year old boys in Desert Hot Springs, California.

PART 1 - INTRODUCTION

FIRST THINGS - WHY ARE DRILLS IMPORTANT?

Reason #1 - It is one of the few ways – maybe even the only way – to deliberately change a baseball swing.

In my 25 years of playing baseball I have had many different coaches who have tried to teach me something new - and this is what I've learned: Trust me when I say a game situation is NOT the time to try to get your body to do something different than what it's been trained to do. It simply won't work, especially when a pitch comes at 95 mph – reflexes WILL take over.

Since what happens at the plate is 99% physical reaction, baseball players use quality repetition to train the body so that the natural reaction is the correct one.

In order to do that, we must practice the proper mechanics over and over again until it becomes our body's natural habit. I like to call that "grooving your swing" (others might call it "muscle memory"). When you can repeat your "A" baseball swing in the games as well as practice, you have successfully grooved your swing.

It is for this reason that quality repetition is a baseball player's best friend, and it is for this reason that baseball drills (even a the simple, Regular Tee Drill) are still used EVERY DAY by hitting legends such as Derek Jeter, Alex Rodriguez, and Albert Pujols.

Reason #2 - One thing at a time

There is another reason that practicing with a batting tee is very important. Even in a controlled environment – such as using a batting tee at 50% speed – you can't focus on changing 10 things at one time.

Each drill is designed to train your body to something very specific. It takes time and many repetitions to work on one aspect of your swing until it becomes natural, and then you can build on that by moving to the next aspect of your swing that needs work.

Reason #3 - Developing a "feel"

Have you ever heard the phrase "paralysis by analysis"? This is one of the most common problems when someone tries to adjust their swing. I know because I've been there many times. This is where you have filled your head with so many mechanical thoughts that you begin to approach each plate appearance mechanically locked up.

Another aspect of "paralysis by analysis" is when you have head knowledge but no "feel". Sometimes the only way to learn what proper mechanics feels like is to see the results and then you'll know you are doing it the right way.

When I was young I taped a square on the garage door of my house and I threw baseballs and tennis balls into that square. I learned to throw accurately by having a feel of what it felt like to throw the ball in that square. I was never taught anything other than basic mechanics for throwing, but because I could throw the ball accurately the mechanics took care of themselves.

I try to apply this same idea to hitting. Hitting can get over analyzed and too mechanical. Many hitters, including myself, have fallen into the trap of "paralysis by analysis." A solid understanding of which drills can help your swing will make you a better hitter while skipping the paralysis.

Hitting drills allow you to isolate an aspect of your swing and then when you hit a line drive to the back of the cage, you know you accomplished what you were trying to do – and you know what it feels like to do it the right way. Then you do it over and over until your body does it naturally. That is the unique thing about a drill... it slows the game down, removing all the extraneous factors and allowing you to isolate exactly what you need to work on.

When you can FEEL what you need to do, and see instant feedback from your results (Did you successfully hit a line drive to the back of the cage?), it translates into solid mechanics that will show up at each plate appearance.

WHAT IS THE BENEFIT TO USING A BATTING TEE?

The batting tee is perhaps the single best training aid a baseball player can use. Here are few reasons why:

1. Repetition is a key to greatness in baseball

Earlier I discussed why getting to the highest levels of the game takes repetition – the best hitters repeat a good baseball swing thousands of times until the correct fundamentals happen without thinking about them. Using a batting tee is one of the best ways to achieve this career-long process. This is why so many Major League baseball players still use the batting tee before games and during off-season – it's not just for young players. The batting tee is a tool players should use from the youth leagues to the Major Leagues.

2. It cuts down on obstacles and distractions

This is the most important reason to use a tee. Using a batting tee allows you to isolate the aspect of your swing that you want to work on.

A tee allows you to swing at 20% or 100%. You are in total control of your swing, which is important for working on weaknesses that make hitting a live pitcher difficult.

You can work on hitting a pitch in a specific location. You can also take a large number of swings in a relatively short amount of time.

3. It allows you to practice on your own time, without a partner or coach

Being a team game, baseball can be difficult to practice without other people around.

Of course, it's great for a coach to watch and critique as you hit off the tee, or to have someone reload the tee for you as you swing, but then you can also go to a cage and practice on your own. It's a beautiful thing.

Since baseball is a game of repetition, using a batting tee will help you achieve your perfect swing through hard work and quality repetition. It also enables you to groove your swing[10] without needing someone's arm to fall off while throwing you batting practice.

4. A batting tee is portable

Most batting tees will fit in your equipment bag or the trunk of your car. Since it's easy to bring with you to the baseball field, batting cage, or backyard net, you will have more opportunities to practice and perfect your game.

TIPS TO GET THE MOST OUT OF YOUR HITTING DRILL PRACTICE

Tip #1 – The ideal contact zone and tee placement.

According to the *Mike Schmidt Study*, you should make contact somewhere between "the toe of your striding foot and the center line[7] of your body" (Schmidt & Ellis, 1994, p. 76). In my 11 years of experience playing professional baseball, I have found this to be true.

If you start getting outside of this zone you will lose power, have less time to see the baseball, or end up hitting foul balls or getting jammed[14].

So what does this mean for batting drills? You should place your batting tee somewhere in this zone for all your drills. The tee will be closer to the center line of your body[7] when hitting an outside pitch, and closer to your front toe on an inside pitch.

Figure 2

Tip #2 – Put a weight on your batting tee.

When using a batting tee especially a portable tee (Figure 2 shows the Tanner Tee and the G Tee), use a 5 or 10 lb. barbell plate to slide over the shaft of the tee. This weight will help keep the tee in place and will keep it from falling over every swing.

Tip #3 – If possible, always do hitting drills in a batting cage or baseball field.

I like to do drills in a batting tunnel or cage that is at least 40 feet long.

The reason I like to hit in a cage is because I get to see how the ball comes off the bat. When hitting into a net it can feel like every ball is hit well. In reality, if you can't see where you hit the ball, you don't really know if you are hitting properly.

You gain a lot of knowledge just by watching the ball come off your bat. When you hit line drives up the middle, you will know you are doing them correctly. Doing these drills on the field is also a good way to see how well and where you are hitting the ball.

Tip #4 – Use the baseball seams as targets.

Place the baseball on the tee with a purpose. For example, if you are trying to hit the inside part of the baseball (which helps you have a better hand path to the baseball, to increase backspin[2] and drive the ball further), place the ball so one seam is facing where you want to make contact.

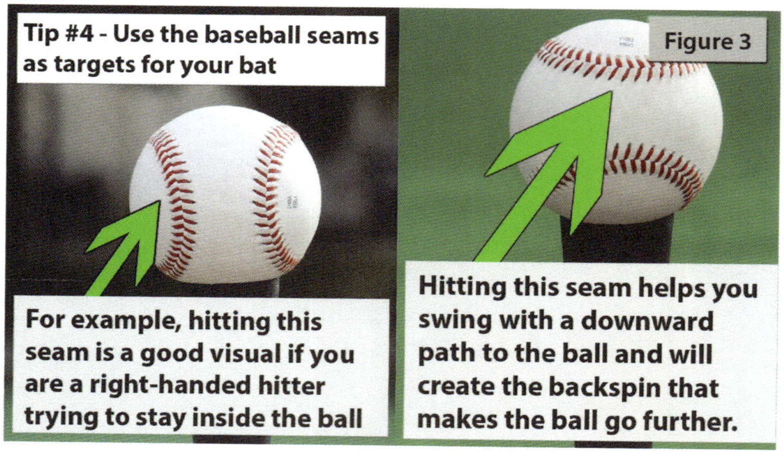

Figure 3

This visual will help you focus on the spot where you want to make contact and it will help guide your swing.

Also, if you are working to get on top of the baseball (to get backspin for greater velocity and distance), set one of the seams in the spot you want to hit (see Figure 3). Use the seam as your target. Most people just place the ball with no thought involved, but this little tip can help get more out of your tee session.

Tip #5 – 7 Absolutes at the point of contact.

There are many different styles of hitting. From batting stance[26] to leg kick, there are many variations of the baseball swing.

However, if you spend enough time watching good hitters, you will notice that there are 7 things which nearly all of them have in common. (Note: There are a few rare exceptions of Major League hitters who do <u>not</u> rotate the back foot every time. I am available through my website ProBaseballinsider.com if you want to explore these exceptions more thoroughly).

These 7 things are the absolutes of hitting mechanics which will provide you with the most powerful and consistent hitting success. As you work to develop your baseball swing through these hitting drills on the batting tee, be mindful and try to achieve these 7 absolutes at contact (Figure 4).

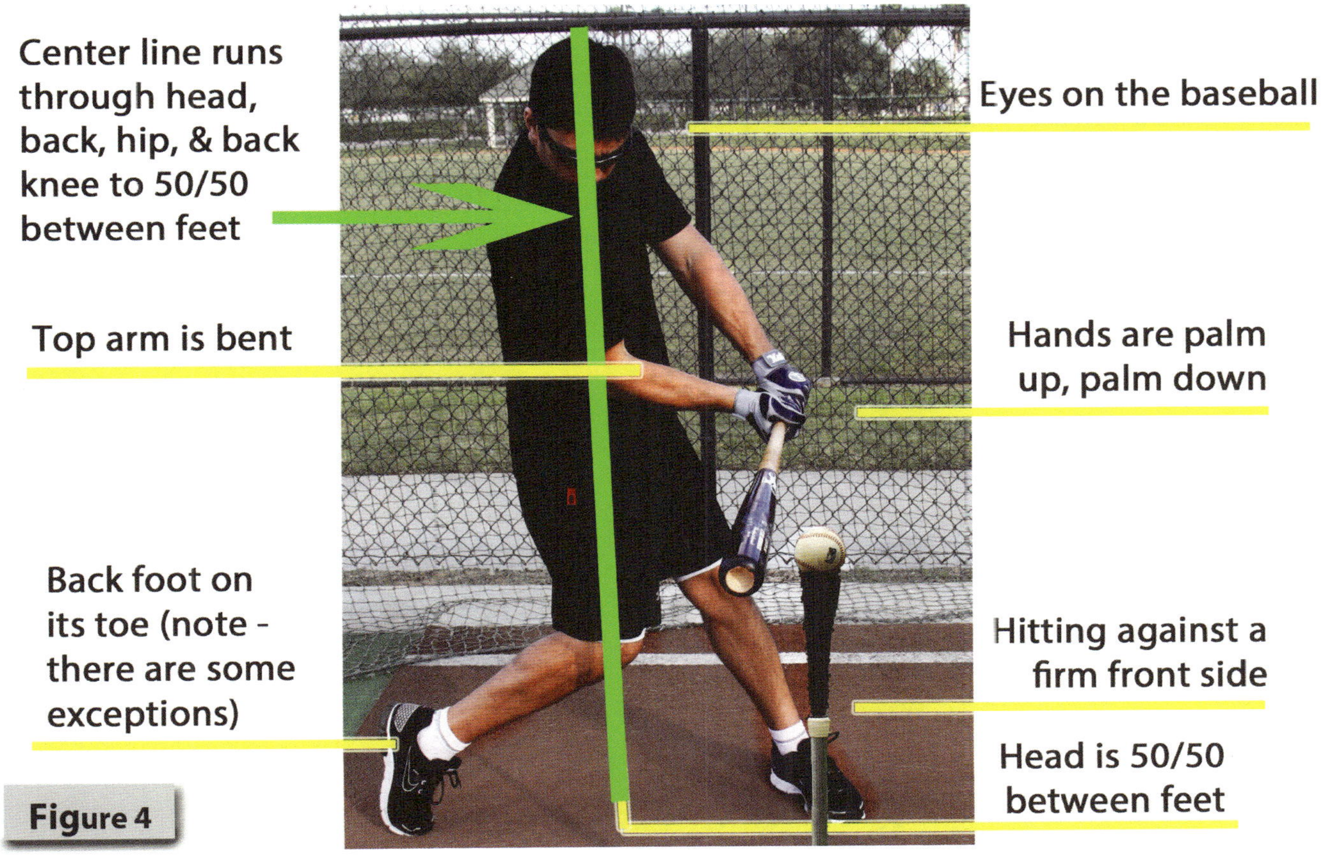

Figure 4

Skill Level / Age Guidelines

Age/Level	*Recommended Drills*
Beginner (under 10 years)	Drill #'s 1, 4, 8, 12, 13,
Intermediate	Drill #'s 1, 4, 5, 6, 7, 8, 9, 12, 13, 16, 18, 19, 20
Advanced (high school/ college/ professional)	Drill #'s 1 – 20; All the drills in this book are useful for advanced-level players

Equipment Used in This Book:

The following chart identifies items you will need to complete these hitting drills. Many of the drills use only a batting tee, while a few others use hitting aids to accomplish specific goals.

Equipment	*# of drills where this item is used*
Baseball bat	20
Batting tee	20
Youth size batting tee (optional)	2 [Low Tee Drill and One Knee Drill]
Extra batting tee (youth or regular size)	4
Baseballs	20
Batting Gloves	20
5 lb. or 10 lb. Barbell weight	20
Short bat	2
Weighted baseball or softball	1
Heavy Bat (optional if you have bat weights)	1
Fungo Bat	1
Bat weights	1 (could be used for all drills)
Basketball or soccer ball	1

***Note** – We provide tips, recommendations and reviews for batting tees and equipment for

- 5 Best batting tees - http://probaseballinsider.com/best-batting-tee/
- Training aids for Hitting Drills - http://probaseballinsider.com/hitting-aids/

PART 2 - YOUR PERSONAL DRILL HELPER

The drills in this book were created to address specific problems or to develop certain skills. If you have any of these common swing problems, there may be a particular drill more helpful to you.

Common Problem	**Drills that will help**
Front shoulder opens up too quickly[9] (trouble reaching the outside pitch)	See drill #2, 3, 8, and 15
Uppercut	4, 6, 7, 8, 13, 14
Wrists roll over[19] too quickly (Hitting too many weak ground balls to pull side)	2, 3, 4, 5, 7, 8, 10, 13, 14, 15, 18, 20
Inconsistent hand path (Not hitting many balls on the barrel)	1, 4, 8, 10, 12, 17, 19
Backside[1] collapses[8] or not getting on back toe at contact (Fouling good pitches straight back); not getting to 50/50 weight distribution	3, 5, 6, 7, 8, 9, 13, 14
Weak swing (i.e. Looking to hit with more power/bat speed)	2, 3, 7, 11, 16, 20
Too stiff (no rhythm)	6, 10, 18, 19
Strike zone judgment	1, 12, 13
Too many swing and misses	1, 2, 4, 8, 15, 17, 19
No separation[20] at contact. Your hands come with you when you stride. They don't stay back. (Weak pop flies to the opposite field)	3, 5, 7, 9, 12, 17, 19
Upper body dominant (Have trouble with low pitch, don't rotate back foot, or can't stay balanced at follow through. Not using legs properly)	5, 7, 9, 11, 16, 20
Getting around the baseball or not staying inside the ball[11]. (Hooking or top spin line drives)	3, 4, 7, 8, 10, 13, 15
Too many pop-ups (may be caused by uppercut or losing the barrel)	3, 4, 6, 9, 10
Unknown problem (these drills either isolate or give instant feedback, which is helpful for diagnosing a swing problem)	2, 3, 4, 5, 9, 19, 20

Note: If you are unsure about terms referring to the baseball bat, check out **Appendix 2 – Anatomy of a Baseball Bat**

PART 3 – DRILLS

******Companion Videos:*** *For instant access to the streaming videos that accompany this book, simply go to http://probaseballinsider.com/freevideo1 and include this code* ***BattingTeeDrills****. Once the form is submitted, you will receive instant access to all 20 videos – one for each drill in this book.*

1 - Regular Tee Drill

Why did I include the Regular Tee Drill in this book? Obviously it's not going to be new to anyone. There are 3 reasons I felt it was important to include in this book:

(1) A reminder to not underestimate the importance of this drill. Too many players and coaches are always look for the latest hitting drill, thinking there is a "magic bullet" out there if only they can find it. However, the reality is that simple, classic drills like this one are used every day by Major League players such as Derek Jeter and Albert Pujols. The reason legendary hitters like these guys still use drills like the Regular Tee Drill is because THEY WORK – if done properly.

(2) This is a batting drill you will likely use for the entire length of your baseball career, so I wanted to provide a few tips for getting the most out of this drill.

(3) To lay out some foundational ideas that apply to ALL the drills in this book.

Summary

As we discussed earlier, being able to repeat your swing is what separates good from great hitters. It seems like an easy concept but it is very difficult to do. The purpose of this drill is to perfect your swing and repeat it over and over, until you can take your adjustments into live batting practice and eventually the game.

Hitting off a tee can be used as a warm up, or as a drill in itself. Either way, it is important to always have a plan when using a tee. It's a great way to get your swing grooved[10] and ready for batting practice or a game.

Purpose:

I love hitting off a tee because it allows me to control the pace of my swing. Even though this is always our goal when you face a pitcher he can sometimes dictate the effort level and pace of our swing.

A tee allows us to slow things down, get back to basics and *focus on making every swing perfect every time*. We can work on pulling a baseball, hitting it the other way. Practice hitting high and low pitches as well as focus on mechanics. Using a tee is a great way to see the spin of the ball off the bat. You can practice your strengths and work to improve on your weaknesses.

Equipment:

- Batting Tee

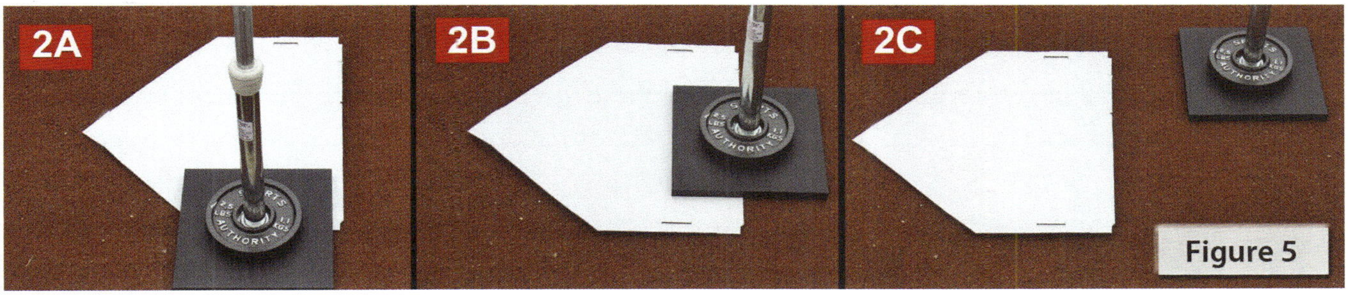

How to Execute this Drill:

1.) ***Setup.*** Always start by addressing home plate where you feel comfortable. Keep the same distance away from the plate so when you move the tee around you will be able to work on pitches you need to be able to hit in games.

2.) ***Practice hitting the outside pitch, 2A.*** When working on hitting the outside pitch you want the ball to travel deeper in the hitting zone so you can take the same swing on an outside pitch as you would an inside pitch. Place the tee a little further back from where you would place it on a pitch down the middle. See how deep you can place the tee to hit the ball the other way. You can start by putting the tee in line with your stomach and then back it up so it's even with your back foot. This is an exaggerated depth, which is helpful because it will act as an indicator to show you how depth affects your swing.

3.) ***Practice for pitches down the middle, 2B.*** Usually for a pitch down the middle the tee should be placed somewhere between where your front foot and stomach end up after you stride. This depth is where you would like to try to hit every pitch that comes down the middle of the plate.

4.) ***Practice hitting the inside pitch, 2C.*** On inside pitches, move the tee in and toward the pitcher by a few inches. You want to make contact with the ball inside a little earlier so your barrel can make contact with the ball without compromising your hands and body positioning. If the inside pitch gets too deep, that's when you get jammed[14] and you won't able to put your strongest swing on the ball.

Checkpoints

Checkpoints for the regular tee drill is to: (1) Have a plan. You are working on whatever it is that you need to work on. (2) Be sure the result is that you are hitting line drives. It's pretty simple. The tee can be one of the greatest hitting aids you will ever use, if you learn to use it properly.

2 - Top Hand, Short bat Drill

Summary

This drill can help you discover a weakness in your swing you didn't know about by showing if the top hand is working like it should; or help to fix a swing that is bottom-hand dominant. If you are bottom-hand dominant, this drill will help you (1) develop more power / bat speed; and (2) develop a better bat path resulting in fewer swing-and-misses.

To be able to hit a line drive, you must be in a strong palm-up position at contact. If you are not doing this successfully, then you will not be able to hit line drives during this exercise. (Note: One handed drills are not recommended for young players, as they may develop bad habits due to lack of strength needed to maintain proper form.)

Purpose

Isolating your top hand[1] uncovers weaknesses that you may not recognize when using two hands. Just like lifting weights, if we always use the barbell to bench press our strong arm takes control. Using dumbbells will make both arms strong. It is the same with hitting.

Your strong hand often takes over during your swing. When you isolate your top hand you will be able to find the strongest spot from which to fire; exactly how your swing path tracks; and how strong or weak you are compared to your other hand. Being the **power hand,** your top hand should work as long as possible facing up and not rolling over[19] until it releases.

The top-hand drill can be humbling at first. But over time you will notice the ball jumping off your bat better and better. Feeling the top hand work individually and getting more proficient with it will definitely make your normal swing better, seem easier, and definitely more powerful. Just by doing this drill your top hand will get stronger.

Figure 6

Drill 2 - Short bat with top hand

Equipment

- Batting Tee
- Short Bat

How to Execute this Drill

Figure 7

1.) Set up the tee for a pitch down the middle of the plate and place a ball on the tee. Start with both hands on the bat and get in your stance[26].
2.) Take your bottom hand[5] off the bat and keep it close to your body, positioned against your chest bone.
3.) Don't move your top hand's place on the bat. Stay choked up, since this is where your hand is normally on a baseball bat. In this drill use your top hand and legs.
4.) Feel your top hand working down through the baseball while you work to hit line drives to the back of the cage.

Checkpoints for Top-Hand, Short Bat Drill

You know you are doing this drill properly if you can…

1.) Swing the bat while keeping your bottom hand[5] still. You may notice a tendency to swing that arm for momentum (see figure 7). This is a no-no. Let your top hand do all the work.

2.) Keep your back elbow tucked close to your body or "in the slot[12]" (figure 8).

Figure 8

3.) Don't allow your wrist to roll over[19] too quickly, which will result in a ground ball to the pull side (figure 9). This drill works well to help you fight that negative tendency.

4.) Make sure you don't dip your backside[1] (figure 10). Fight to avoid swinging up and creating lift. These movements will not work when you need to catch up to a fastball.

If you are dipping back and or swinging up, you should be able to feel this movement during the drill and you will definitely see it by where the ball ends up. Isolating your top hand will help you feel how your body works together with your swing.

5.) Hit line drives! The biggest indicator as to whether you are doing this drill properly is RESULTS. When you start to see line drives up the middle, it indicates that you are successfully hitting with your top-hand palm up through the hitting zone. Once you get that feel and see those line drives your swing is getting grooved[10].

Figure 9

Checkpoint 4: Rolling your wrist too early loses power

Figure 10

Checkpoint 4: don't dip your back side

3 - Bottom-hand, Short bat Drill

Summary

The purpose of the bottom-hand, short-bat drill (figure 11) is to isolate your bottom hand[5] so you can have an understanding how it should work in your swing. Using the bottom hand[5] independently will make it stronger and will make your two hand swing more efficient and powerful.

If you have difficulty with this drill at first, it means this is exactly the drill you should be working on. Strengthening your bottom hand can help to fix problems like rolling your wrists over too early (which causes you to hit ground balls or pull foul too often) and too many swings-and-misses (caused an over-active top hand pulling the bat out of the zone too soon).

Purpose

As I talked about in the previous drill, when you lift weights it is important to isolate individual limbs so they can independently get strong. The same idea is true with the baseball swing.

When you develop the proper feel for your bottom hand[5] and can hit line drives, it will be easier to do with two hands. The pulling action of your bottom hand is what starts your pull to the baseball. Since most people are top hand dominant (since it is usually the throwing hand), we tend to take over our swing too early with that top hand.

Being familiar with the role of your bottom hand will help you better understand your swing as a whole, and will help you recognize when adjustments are needed.

This drill takes out all the unnecessary movements of your swing. With one hand you are not strong enough to be anything but efficient, so it will help shorten your swing[22]. Once you can feel strong with one hand, swinging with two should be no problem.

Equipment:

- Batting Tee
- Short Bat

Figure 11

How to Execute this Drill:

1.) Set up the tee for a pitch down the middle of the plate. Place a ball on the tee. Start with both hands on the bat and get in your stance.
2.) Take your top hand off the bat and keep it close to your body positioned against your chest bone.
3.) Swing using your bottom hand[5] and legs. Keep your top hand still. The tendency is to swing your arm to get some momentum. Avoid this tendency and be deliberate about making your bottom hand do all the work.

Checkpoints:

1.) Swing down through the ball (See figure 10). Make sure you don't dip your backside[1] and swing up through the baseball.
2.) Don't lift your front elbow dragging your barrel trying to get lift (figure 12). You will feel the difference. Remember you need to swing down in the game, so swinging up during this drill will do nothing for your two handed swing.
3.) Feel the front side pulling to start your swing and feel the torque you can create with your front side.
4.) As I said before, the biggest indicator of doing this drill properly is RESULTS, so an important checkpoint is to hit line drives back up the middle.

Figure 12

4 - High Tee Drill

Summary

Hitting too many pop flies? Want to hit more powerful line drives? Trouble with pitches up in the zone? This is a great drill to help with these things, and it's one you'll want to keep in your tool box throughout your baseball career.

It can be particularly difficult to hit down on the baseball on a high pitch. The tendency is to swing up to the baseball, which translates into a pop-up or a miss in the game because of the added velocity. If you normally collapse[3] your backside[1], this drill will help you stay strong and tall on your back leg.

This drill is also great for working on putting proper backspin on the baseball. When you swing down on the ball you create backspin making the ball travel further. This is much more difficult to do on a high pitch. This drill forces good habits on a tough pitch, making you less likely to miss those few good pitches you get in the games.

Purpose

As you start facing pitchers that have good velocity (90 mph +) this posture of being strong and tall on your back leg is very important. It is easy to get by with sub par mechanics when a pitcher isn't throwing hard, but as the velocity kicks up, you need to have better mechanics.

It is a natural tendency to swing up at a high pitch. When we do this, if we hit the ball it is usually a weak fly ball somewhere. This drill will force you, by using your legs, to get on top of the ball and hit a hard line drive.

Statistically, most swing and misses are below the ball on fastballs, so this is an important drill for helping us to make contact more consistently and with better outcomes.

Figure 13

Equipment

- Batting Tee
- Bucket or Chair (Needed ONLY IF your batting tee won't extend up to chest level)

How to Execute this Drill

1.) Set the tee up for a pitch down the middle of the plate. Now raise the tee to its highest point. You want it to be somewhere between your chest and chin height. If the tee doesn't allow you to raise it this high, place the tee on a bucket or chair to get the ideal height for this drill.

2.) Swing - Take this high pitch and hit a line drive head height to the back of the cage.

Checkpoints

If you can get the ball to travel 40-70 feet in the air at the same height it was set up on the tee, you accomplished the goal of the drill. Being able to do this makes you get on top of the baseball and to create the perfect line drive you need to get great backspin[2].

5 - Net Tee Drill

Summary

This drill is useful for shortening[21] your hand path to the baseball by keeping your hands close to your body and forcing you to stay inside the ball[11]. This will eliminate casting your barrel[6] and force you to stay tight[27] and compact, which makes for a more efficient swing. In other words, this drill will help develop power (through better bat speed AND putting proper backspin on the baseball – more on this below), and will also help if you are experiencing too many swings-and-misses or fouling good pitches back.

Benefits of this drill

1.) More Power. If you are not hitting hard line drives as consistently as you would like (such as too many hooking line drives that don't have the distance they should) , it is probably because you are not getting the proper backspin on the baseball. This drill will help you attack the inside part of the ball, which is the only way to create that backspin. Just to be clear, hitting the inside of the baseball does NOT necessarily mean hitting the ball the other way. The hooking line drives are caused by getting out and around the baseball (i.e. casting your barrel) and creating sidespin by hitting the outside part of the ball. The benefit putting proper backspin on the baseball is that it will travel further.

Bat speed is another critical aspect of power. The shorter the distance of your hand path, the tighter the axis of rotation will be. This results in greater leverage and acceleration of the bat (i.e. bat speed). A long, inefficient swing loses bat speed and therefore results in less power. This drill causes you to shorten your hand path to the baseball for maximum bat speed.

2.) Better bat path. Weak ground balls or choppers to the pull side are usually caused by a poor path to the baseball.

There is a tendency to swing around the baseball instead of staying inside it and driving through it. This drill is needed because it will shorten your swing[22] by helping you stay tight[27] with your hands to your body and removing unnecessary movement. All of this benefits you by making your rotation to the ball quicker. This will give you that better path to the ball.

3.) More time to see the pitch. Another benefit of a good bat path is that you gain a few more precious milliseconds to see the ball before starting your swing. If your swing is shorter, faster, more efficient, then you will have a little more time to see the ball – giving you more time to identify the pitch and react appropriately.

4.) Teaches Pulling the ball correctly. This drill is also great for teaching players to pull the ball correctly. Many hitters when pulling a baseball get their hands away from their body and get around the ball with their barrel, this promotes ground balls and hooking fly balls, both of which are not ideal.

This drill shows you how to stay inside and drive the ball to the pull side with backspin (If you remember from Tip 4, backspin makes the ball go farther). As you will find out, staying tight[27] with your swing is what you are trying to accomplish every time. This drill will help you accomplish that feel.

Equipment

- Batting Tee
- Batting Cage Net (You could use a fence but if and when you hit the fence it will ding up your bat and it may hurt wrists depending on how hard you hit it.)

How to execute this drill:

1. From your normal spot in the batting cage, walk forward until you're 30-35 inches from the net. You can measure by placing the knob of your bat so its touching your stomach and the end of your bat is barely grazing the net (see Figure 14.A).
2. Once you have set your distance from the net, place the tee where it feels comfortable - without backing up from the net.
3. Swing without hitting the net. It's ok if you lightly graze the net, but if the net starts interfering with the swing, you know you need get your hands more linear and inside (Figure 14.B).

Checkpoints

Use these checkpoints to make sure you are getting the most benefit from this drill.

1.) Hit line drives up the middle to the pull side of the cage without hitting the net. When you are doing this consistently you know your bat path is correct.

Figure 14.B
Working on proper bat path: Swing without hitting the net

2.) If you are hitting the net, work to keep your hands close to your body and finish your swing. Once again, it's ok if you brush the net, but if you get too much of the net during your swing, it will stop your bat.
3.) You are trying to take a good quality swing (start at 50% effort level if you find this drill difficult) by taking your normal stride and using your backside[1] to start your swing.
4.) It is important not to cheat. Check your stride to ensure you are not stepping away from the plate.
5.) After you swing check to make sure you are not falling away from the net. If you find yourself off balance after contact, it probably means you were cheating to avoid the net by leaning away during your swing.

6 - Step Through Drill

Summary

The Step Through Drill (Figure 15) is useful if you feel stuck on your backside[1]. This drill will help you feel the linear movement you need in your swing. It forces you to use your backside and legs together to finish on your back toe (or even slightly off the ground).

This drill also helps you get to separation[20] and feel your hands work. You will feel your body step away from your hands thus getting into a strong separation when your front foot hits the ground. Your hands will be back and you will feel tension in your front side.

Purpose

(1.) This drill is important because we hear many coaches say, "stay back." Many people have a hard time explaining or understanding what that even means, but it can get interpreted as "squash the bug[25]" (spinning on the back leg without any linear forward motion[16]). We want to rotate on our back leg and finish on our toe, while getting through or even off of our backside[1]. This is where our power comes from, and this drill helps us feel the proper linear movement[16] we need during our swing (which keeps our bat in the zone longer and improves our odds of making quality contact with the pitch).

(2.) This drill also helps with developing rhythm. Hitting needs a rhythm to keep us in motion. It is easier to start a swing if we have a little movement than from a dead stand still. If we get too mechanical our rhythm is the first thing to leave our swing. Having rhythm keeps us relaxed longer, and when we are relaxed longer we can whip the bat[31] quicker.

Keeping your muscles tension-free prevents putting your body into a "crisis management mode that forces the bulkier muscles to take over. Though the bulkier muscles are important in a motion, if they dominate, the motion will lock, and be, forced and awkward." (Yellin and Biancalana, 2010, p.16). The bottom line is, tense muscles are slower – slower to react to the pitch, and slower in overall bat speed (i.e. less whip = less power).

(3.) If you are having problems achieving proper separation[20] or getting your hands back, this

Figure 15

drill helps. You will feel your hands get back into a strong position, once your front foot hits the ground you will feel tension in your front oblique. From this position you are ready to swing.

Equipment

- Batting Tee

How to execute this drill

1.) ***Setup*** - Set the tee up for a pitch down the middle of the plate. Instead of getting in your normal stance[26] back up a foot or so (in the direction of the catcher). Face home plate.
2.) ***Step right*** –(If you are a left-handed hitter, you'll start by stepping with your left foot). Start by taking a step with your back foot and place it in the batter's box in the same place you would dig in for an at bat. Make sure your back foot is square[24] to home plate.
3.) ***Step left*** - Now take your other leg and stride into a hitting position.
4.) ***Swing*** - Use the rhythm you have created with your legs to finish your swing.
5.) ***Follow-through*** - After you swing your follow through should allow for your back foot to either be off the ground or on its toe **(Optional Ending 1)**. Make sure you finished balanced with your chest finishing towards the pitcher. Refer to Figure 15.

Step while thinking about your bottom half[4]. At the same time, keep your hands relaxed and once you take your stride you should be able to feel your hands get back into a strong position.

Variation of the drill: For hitters that are still having trouble feeling the linear movement[16] that is necessary in a swing, or can't get away from "squashing the bug[25]," add this extra movement to the end of this drill. This will force you to over exaggerate getting off of your back toe, forcing you to throw your back leg at the baseball.

Once you have made contact and are starting your follow through, take your back knee and drive it up towards the pitcher **(Optional Ending 2).** Get the knee up to waist height.

This over exaggerated movement will force you to use your back leg with a linear movement[16] and learn to stay balanced while driving into your front leg.

Goal Checkpoints:

1. Hit line drives up the middle.
2. After you finished your swing, see if your back foot was in the air or on its toe at contact.
3. Make sure you finish with your chest towards the pitcher; this will show you are getting off of your backside[1] properly.

As you are striding, hopefully your hands are getting into the strong position I mentioned earlier. This should happen automatically during this drill. You want to feel your hands working together with your lower half, just remember to keep them relaxed.

7 - Weighted Baseball or Softball Drill

Summary

This drill will help you hit through the baseball by using strong hip rotation and lower body power. It will ensure you are in a strong position at contact and will help increase strength in your hands and forearms.

Purpose

It is very important to groove your swing[10] not to just hit the baseball but to drive **through** the baseball. Driving through the ball with this drill encourages strong hip rotation and lower body explosion to hit the ball. This drill will help increase your power and explosion during your swing. It's a good drill for getting your legs involved.

This drill also makes sure you are in a strong hitting position at contact. When hitting a heavier object than a baseball you will begin to feel the bat slow down or even recoil once you make contact.

Through repetition you will begin to find where you feel strongest with your base[3] and hands, as well as finding out your strongest position in your swing. You will also get quite a workout with your forearms and hands. Once you go back to hitting a baseball it will feel like a whiffle ball.

Equipment

1. Batting Tee
2. Weighted Baseballs or Softballs (they range from 9 oz. to 32 oz. A regular baseball is 5 oz.)

How to Execute this Drill

Set up the tee for a pitch down the middle of the plate. Place the weighted softball or basketball on the tee and hit normally. This is a **feel drill**, that means that you will learn a lot about your swing through the repetition of this drill.

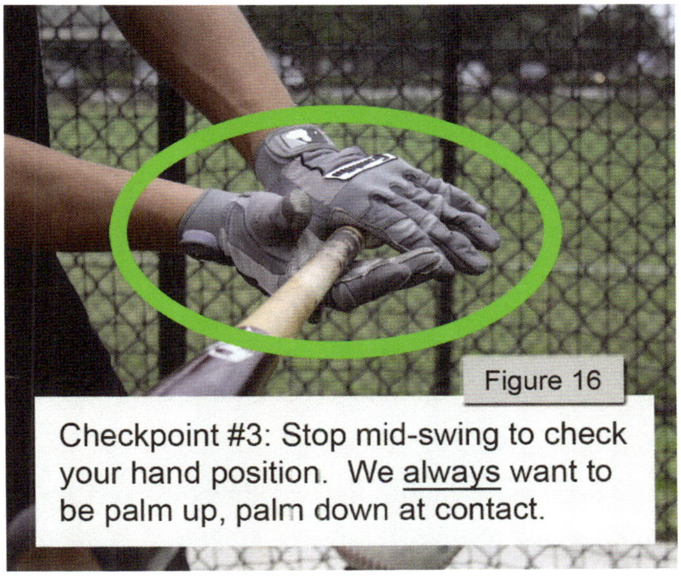

Figure 16

Checkpoint #3: Stop mid-swing to check your hand position. We always want to be palm up, palm down at contact.

Checkpoints:

1.) Hit the weighed softball or basketball up the middle. Don't try to do too much with the ball.

2.) Concentrate on hitting through the ball. Over time you will feel stronger and will be able to see the results when you go back to hitting a baseball.

3.) This is a good time to check if your hands are in the strongest possible position at contact.. Just before you hit the ball, stop and check that your hands are in the palm up, palm down[18] position (see figure 16).

8 – Two ball, Two tee Drill

Summary

This drill is helpful for hitters who are having trouble getting off their back side, spinning off the ball instead of driving through it, or pulling most pitches. If you swing and miss a lot or have trouble with the outside pitch, this is a great drill.

Purpose

This drill helps with the problems I just mentioned because it teaches two very important hitting skills: (1) Hitting *through* the baseball; and (2) Keeping the bat in the zone longer.

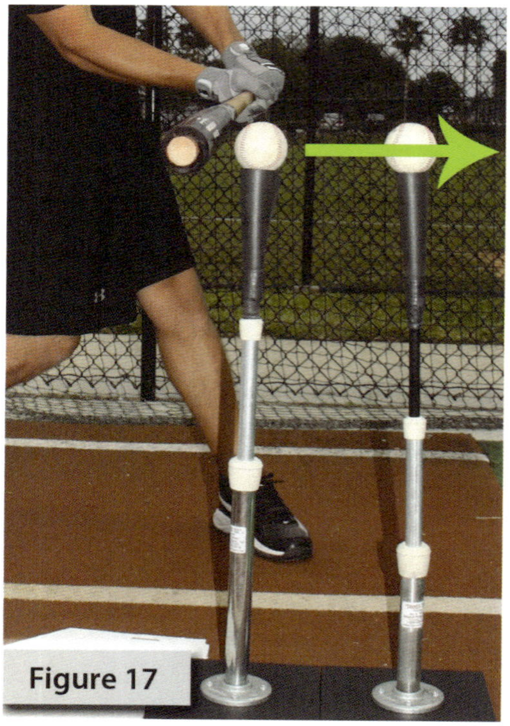
Figure 17

Once you make contact, you need to hit "through" the baseball (see Figure 17). There are many hitters that start their finish as soon as they make contact. If you are not hitting *through* the ball, then your bat is not transferring the full force of its momentum into the baseball. Hitting through the ball is also important for creating that optimal backspin[2] that gives line drives more pop and distance.

Starting your finish too soon also makes your bat quick in and quick out of the hitting zone, which makes hitting even more difficult than it already is. Staying in the zone longer means your window of opportunity for making solid contact with the baseball is just a little bit more forgiving. In my experience, having those extra split seconds with your bat in the zone translates into more hits.

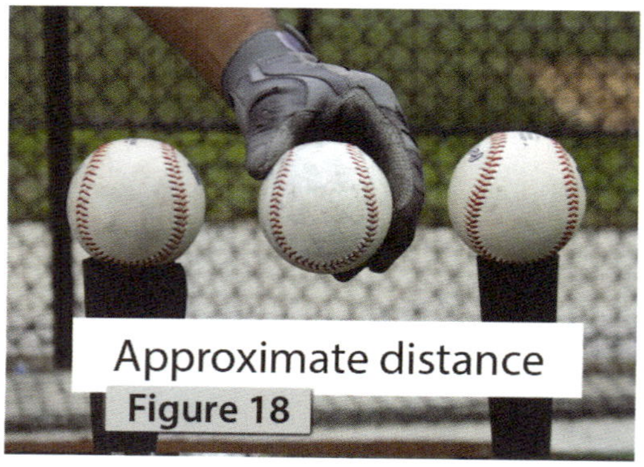

Figure 18

This drill will force you to not only hit the baseball but to focus on hitting through it to the next ball, giving you a very effective *mental image* and *feel* for what you are trying to achieve in your swing during the games.

This bat action and visualization helps you to stay on pitches when they have late movement.

Equipment

- Two Batting Tees

How to Execute this Drill

1.) Address home plate how you normally would in a game. Place the tee for a pitch down the middle of the plate.
2.) Take the next tee and place it as close as possible to the first tee so it is a direct line between the first tee and the pitcher's mound.
3.) Place a ball on both tees. As a hitter you are looking at the first tee with a ball on top. There will be a gap between the two tees that would be close to the diameter of a baseball (see Figure 18). Now you are set up properly for this drill.
4.) Swing. When you swing, you will hit both baseballs (hopefully up the middle, but they are going to scatter once they hit each other). Having the visual of hitting the balls on the tee will help you develop a better swing path by working the bat "long through the baseball."

Checkpoints

Feel is a very important part of this drill. The idea is to swing the bat and not only hit the first ball, but take the barrel through the first ball, through the gap, and through the second ball. This is the feel we want when hitting the baseball during a regular at-bat.

9 - High Back Tee Drill

Summary

This is a great hand path drill. It will help you to stay "short to the ball[21]" up until contact by keeping the barrel above your hands.

Figure 19

To hit the ball you need to take your hands down to the ball (eliminating the "upper cut"), stay tight[27] to your body with your hands, and it will make you deliver your barrel at the most ideal time so you are in the hitting zone for as long as possible without giving up bat speed.

Purpose

When it comes to hitting mechanics, some of the most common problems are (1) losing the barrel[17] and (2) dipping the backside[8]. These mechanical flaws make for a longer swing path, which slows down your bat speed.

A common baseball phrase "short to and long through" explains how we need to be short[21] getting "to" the baseball and then hit "through" the baseball. This drill forces your barrel to stay above your hands until the last possible second when you can drop the barrel into the hitting zone, thus staying on top of the baseball.

Figure 20

This is a great drill to try even when you don't feel like you have a long swing. Setting it up and hitting will instantly give you feedback regarding your swing (Incidentally, this is one reason I like drills so much - because it takes the analyzing out of hitting). This drill can be very helpful for shortening[21] and making your swing more efficient[22].

Equipment

- Two Batting Tees
- Bucket (only needed if your tee won't extend high enough)

How to Execute this Drill

1.) ***Front tee*** - Take one tee and set it up how you would normally. Keep in mind the lower you set the tee the more difficult the drill is to execute. Keep the height of the tee fairly normal, don't get too extreme either way in its height. Also, the inside pitches are going to be easier to hit than the outside pitches in this drill, but it will force you to keep your hands tight[27] to your body so you don't make contact with the back tee.

2.) ***Back tee*** - Take the 2nd tee and line it up directly behind the point of home plate positioned about 1 to 5 inches behind your back foot (Figure 19). How far it is behind your back foot depends on how difficult the drill is for you. Once the back tee is in place raise it as high as it can go. If the tee doesn't extend very high you can always place it on a bucket. The ideal height is somewhere between your chest and face.

3.) ***Swing and adjustments*** - Hit line drives without hitting the back tee (Figure 21). If you keep hitting this tee, move it back a bit, if you don't hit it at all, try moving it a little closer to the plate. The small movement makes the drill much more difficult.

Checkpoints

1. You want to swing and hit the ball on the front tee without making contact with the back tee. To avoid hitting the back tee, you have to keep your hands and barrel close to your body as the barrel stays above your hands. Once you are past the back tee, let the barrel fly.
2. When you produce line drives, you know this drill was done correctly. When you can hit line drives on inside and outside pitches you are teaching your body to deliver the barrel to the hitting zone at the right time.

Figure 21

10 – Separation Drill

Summary

This drill is helpful for someone dealing with balance problems, trouble with getting to ideal separation[26], and/or trouble achieving a level swing.

Purpose

This drill helps with three key elements that easily become common problems to any hitter: (1) balance, (2) separation[20], and (3) a level swing. The purpose of this drill is to slow your swing down into these 3 different stages, focusing on each stage.

A couple seasons ago, I wasn't feeling good at the plate and my results showed it. This drill helped me get back on track. I actually used it in the games for a couple weeks until I started feeling good again.

The Separation Drill is also helpful when trying to slow your body down and build rhythm throughout your swing. In other words, until the explosion part of your swing, you want to be as slow (i.e. relaxed, smooth, rhythmic, etc.) as possible. When you get tense, your body will be slower to react, your bat speed will suffer, and you will have more trouble reading the pitch because your head is moving around too much.

I love this drill because I feel so locked in when I do it and I feel I can hit a line drive every time. Your lower half is your base and the foundation for your swing. If it is working properly, then it allows your hands and everything else to work properly as well.

Equipment

- Batting Tee

How to Execute this Drill

1. Set up the tee for a pitch down the middle of the plate. To properly execute this drill you need to put emphasis on three stages of this drill.
2. ***Stage 1 – Balance.*** Start in your normal batting stance, addressing home plate. Take your front foot and place it so it's touching your back foot, both are square to home plate[24].
3. With your bat resting on your back shoulder and your hands relaxed, gently lift your front knee like a pitcher and hold this position when the knee gets parallel with the ground. Hold this position for a second or two.
4. ***Stage 2 – Separation.*** Take your leg that is raised and make a controlled stride to your normal stride length. At the same time take your bat from resting on your back shoulder and move hands back

away from your body. This should happen at the same time as you take your stride. This movement should feel like you are striding away from your hands, as a result your head and body shouldn't move forward much if at all.

5. Once your front foot lands, make sure that your weight is evenly distributed 50/50 at this point. Hold this position for a second or two. You should be able to feel tightness in your front side creating a rubber band type effect.

   This stretch (the result of correct separation[20]) is important for a powerful explosion that results in good bat speed during the next stage of your swing. If your separation[20] is correct, it will be a BIG help for stage 3 – a level swing.

6. ***Stage 3 - Level swing.*** The great thing about this stage is that once you are in a perfect 50/50 stance with your hands back in a strong hitting position (from stage 2), the level swing happens naturally. The 3rd stage is a direct result of the first two being done correctly.

   It is important when you start your swing that you don't recoil to get a little extra on your swing. Just swing from the position you are in. It should almost feel like your hands are just swinging because your base is already in a good position.

Checkpoints

The goal is to be able to hit line drives and have the swing feel almost effortless. This should be the result after stage 3.

1.) Check yourself after the "balance" stage so that you aren't falling all over the place when you pick your knee up.

2.) Check yourself once you get to the "separation[20]" stage to make sure your hands are back and your weight distribution is 50/50. The even weight distribution at this point of the swing allows for an easier level swing. If we have too much weight on our back side at this point we will be forced to swing "up hill", using our hands to compensate for poor leg positioning. Getting to a good 50/50 weight distribution will allow for an effortless swing. Once you feel that and can hit line drives to all fields, you know this drill is working.

11 - Inside Tee Drill

Summary

This drill is NOT just meant to help you hit the inside pitch. The Inside Tee drill helps players develop the proper form and bat path that will make you a better hitter for any type of pitch. It is designed to keep you inside the baseball[11] by emphasizing the first movement of the swing.

- This drill is perfect for those who are constantly out in front of off-speed pitches and hit most balls to the pull side.
- Also, this drill will help players who swing and miss more than they should, because it's designed to keep your barrel in the hitting zone longer.

You will start driving more balls in the opposite field gap as well as be able to pull off speed pitches the correct way with authority.

Purpose

The Inside Tee Drill is needed because our initial move to the baseball needs to be the same every time, no matter the pitch or location. This first movement is often called "getting your elbow in the slot[12]."

This is a drill that many professionals use before batting practice to warm up. Being able to do this helps is many ways.

1. You can aggressively hit fastballs to the opposite gap and at the same time have established the position necessary to pull an off speed pitch.
2. More ground balls are hit to the pull side than to the opposite field, so being able to stay inside the baseball[11] will cut down on rolling over[19] to the pull side and hopefully get more line drives that get through the infield.
3. You will get better backspin[2] on the baseball. Once you lose your barrel[17] too early and get around the ball you are creating a hooking (or topspin[29]) action. Staying inside the baseball[11] will get you better backspin allowing you to hit the ball further.
4. When you can stay inside the baseball[11], you will be in position to hit the pitch at any location. The pitch away where you may

have swung and missed or rolled over before is now a line drive the other way.

5. Your mental approach is much better, which gets more important as you move up levels and the pitchers get better. You may only get one good pitch to hit every at bat. You must give yourself every opportunity not to miss it.
6. Now because your swing is tighter if you see the inside fastball early it is easier to get the barrel to the pitch the right way and pull the ball with backspin[2].

This move starts by pulling the knob of the bat to the inside part of the baseball. As this is happening your back elbow is getting close to your body (in the slot[12]) keeping your hands close.

To attack an inside pitch you must keep your hands and barrel inside the ball[11] until the barrel reaches the hitting zone.

For this drill, your goal hit the ball off the inside tee up the middle or to the opposite field. To accomplish this, you will have to keep your hands very tight to your body. While this drill forces you to stay slightly more inside than you would in a game, it is very helpful to correct the tendency of casting your barrel[6].

Equipment

- Batting Tee

How to Execute this Drill

1.) Address home plate as you normally would in a game.
2.) Take the batting tee and place it on the inside half of the plate.
3.) Shift the depth of the tee to where your front knee is after you take your stride.
4.) Move the tee further in and further back (towards the catcher) to make this drill more difficult.
5.) Take a normal swing and hit a line drive up the middle or to the opposite field.

Checkpoints

1. Fight to stay inside the baseball[11]. By over exaggerating and fighting to stay inside the ball[11], you are teaching your body many good movements towards a perfect swing without having to think too hard about your swing mechanics.
2. Fight to hit through the ball with your body. It is common to try to create more space[23] by recoiling your upper body so you are pulling away from the ball (Fig 23). Fight against this and use your hands.

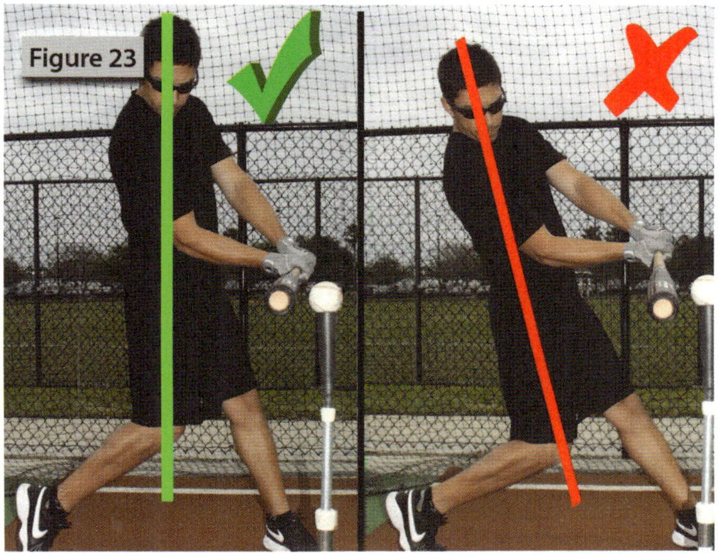
Figure 23

12 - Low Tee Drill

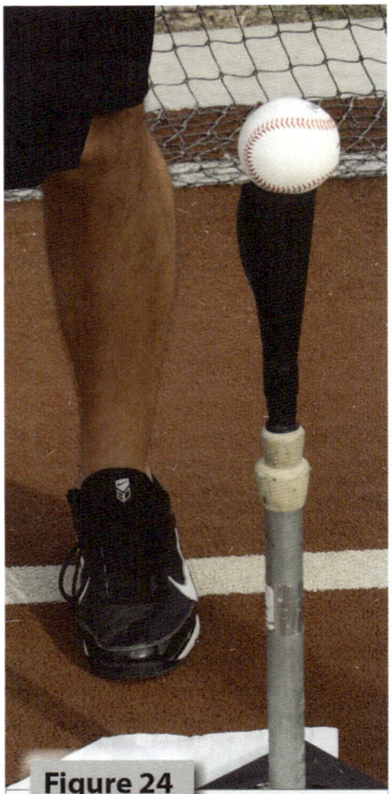

Figure 24

Low Tee Drill
The tee is set as low as it will go

Summary

This drill is helpful for the person that hits choppers and weak ground balls to the infielders. I know everyone does this but if you feel you do this too much this drill may be helpful.

Also, if you are a hitter with a flat bat[13] at the launch position[15] or have a narrow stance[26] it can be difficult to handle low pitches. Even though you want to hit to your strength, since every pitcher is trying to keep the ball down, it is helpful to be able to handle low pitches in the game.

Purpose

There are two reasons why the Low Tee Drill is helpful.

Reason #1 - Working on hitting a low pitch off a tee really makes you use your legs in your swing.

Sometimes it is difficult to explain exactly how to use your legs, but when you can find a drill that forces you to do it, it will allow you to know exactly what it should feel like.

When hitters start thinking a lot about mechanics it can cause "paralysis by analysis." When this occurs it is very common for the hitter to stop using their legs in their swing and get very upper body dominate. Why? I don't know, but I know that this drill will force you to use your base and understand how important it is for your swing.

Reason #2 - It forces you to hit the low pitch the right way. Once your legs get you into an optimal position, you want to drop the barrel to the baseball. Without these two pieces working together, our heads end up being a long distance from the contact point.

We need to use our legs to get into our stance and drive through the ball, not just hit choppers into the ground. As I stated before that hitters with a flat bat[13] at the launch position[15] or have a narrow stance may handle the high pitch better than the low one. Working off a low tee will help you feel how your body needs to work to handle this pitch.

Equipment

- Batting Tee (one that can get to about knee height; or a youth-size batting tee)

How to Execute this Drill

1.) Address home plate as you would in a game. Take the batting tee and set it up for a pitch down the middle of the plate.
2.) Make the tee as low as possible.
3.) Place a ball on the tee and swing. When you swing, GET LOW! Don't just reach your arms for the baseball. Get your head and legs low and attack it. Your arms should be bent and your elbow in the slot[12] (tight against your side). If you have straightened your elbow and find yourself reaching, you may as well go eat some potato chips because the drill isn't doing anything for you.
4.) You can move the tee around to simulate pitches away, in, and down the middle but make sure to focus and be able to handle the pitch down the middle.

Checkpoints

Hit a line drive head height to the back of the cage. This drill takes some time to get used to. When I struggle with this drill, I hit ground balls. Then, trying to compensate, I usually hit underneath the ball and pop it up. Once you get the feel of not just hitting but blasting a line drive up the middle you will really be able to feel your legs work and understand how to hit that pitch in actual games.

Figure 25

Low Tee Drill - Don't be lazy and reach for the ball. Use your legs to get low and then attack it.

13 - Inside and Outside Tee Drill

Summary

This drill can help with strike zone awareness and gives us confidence that we can handle the pitch in and away. If you struggle with your plate coverage and knowing exactly what you can and can't hit, this drill will help you to lock in on the strike zone.

Purpose

Every hitter will have at bats where you see a pitch out of the pitchers hand and you know it is too far away and will be called a ball… until the ball gets closer and hits the outside corner for a strike. You feel helpless because it seemed too far away for you to hit.

This drill gives you the visual of the outside and inside pitch at the same time, improving strike zone awareness. This drill will also give you confidence that by being able to hit the inside and outside strike off the tee, it will be able to transfer in the game. Once you know you have proper plate coverage no pitch should haunt you. Now you just need to swing at strikes, because this drill shows you that you can handle any strike.

Equipment

- Two Batting Tees

Setup & Execution

1.) ***Position yourself.*** To set up for this drill first address home plate as you would in a game.

2.) ***1st tee.*** Take the first tee and place it on the inside corner of the zone and just outside where your front foot lands after your stride (see Figure 25).

3.) ***2nd tee.*** Take the second tee and place it on the outside corner and have it somewhere between your stomach and front knee after you stride. Also, make sure the outside tee is a bit higher than the inside tee. (If it were the other way around you would make contact with the inside tee trying to hit the outside tee).

Figure 26

Setup for
Drill 13 - Inside & outside tee

4.) ***Helper or alternate.*** Ideally, it's best to have someone help you out with this drill. You would take your stride and pause, your helper would say "inside" or "outside" and then you would hit that corresponding ball. If you don't have a helper, take your stride, pause, then alternate between pitches. Make sure that after you swing that your stride foot is in the same place every time.

Know your place. Move around in the batter's box until you feel perfect plate coverage for the inside and outside pitch. Once you find this spot, make sure you can get to this spot every time either by measuring with your bat from the plate, tap the outside part of the plate or whatever helps you.

Your spot in the batter's box may be different than the "community hole" every person uses in the batter's box. Know where your spot is every time, get there and then trust yourself.

Checkpoints

1.) Don't cheat by stepping towards the outside pitch and away from the inside pitch. The pause in this drill helps to stop the unwanted "cheating" in this drill.

2.) During your pause you can also look to the ball you are not going to hit. Make sure in your mind that you could hit it before you swing at the other tee location. Seeing the ball on the tee will give you a good visual of the strike zone and you will see how well you can handle each pitch.

3.) Make sure that after you swing that your stride foot is in the same place every time.

Figure 26.B

Stride and then pause - from this position, you can reach the insider OR the outside tee.
Notice that the feet are in the exact same spot for both pitch locations.

14 - Inverted Top Hand Drill

Summary

This drill is helpful to the hitter that has an overactive top hand[30]. If you pull a lot of hard foul balls, it can mean your top hand takes over too quickly. This drill will help your bottom hand[5] take control until it is time for the top hand to get involved. It will give you just enough top hand at certain points in your swing.

You will learn to push through the baseball with the top hand[30] but pull with your bottom hand[5] all the way to your one handed finish. This drill is good for isolating your bottom hand and teaching it how to work together with an overactive top hand.

Purpose

This drill is useful for people that pull a lot of hard foul balls. Even though you are hitting the ball hard and keep telling yourself its just your timing, it may be more than that. Obviously you are seeing the ball well enough to hit it hard but if you get a good pitch to handle and crush it foul, there is a mechanical flaw. Most times it is from a top hand[30] that kicks in too quickly.

If you have this problem, you probably handle the high pitch well and occasionally you will take a low pitch and hit it off of your shin. This is common and this drill gets your bottom hand[5] to become more aggressive so your top hand[30] can wait just a split second longer to take over. We get our power from our top hand and we need it, but it has to work at the right time or we waste the power it provides.

This drill also keeps us linear[16] with our upper body making us work up the middle and hopefully turning our hard hit foul line drives into rockets up the middle.

Equipment

- Batting Tee

How to Execute this Drill

1.) ***Position tee.*** Set up the tee for a pitch down the middle of the plate. Address home plate the same way you would in a game.

2.) ***Narrow stance.*** Leave your back foot where it is and move your front foot so your stance[26] is shoulder width (narrower than normal for most people) and your feet are square to home plate[24].

3.) ***Invert your top hand.*** Take your grip on the bat and now take your top hand[30] off and turn it upside down so your thumbs from your bottom and top hand are now touching (Fig 27).

4.) ***Ready position – Top hand loose, elbow high.*** Your back elbow will be high and your top hand is not fully wrapped around the handle. It should feel like you can throw the bat with your top hand while you are still holding on with your bottom hand.

5.) ***Swing and <u>push</u> with your top hand.*** Don't grab the bat when you swing – see Figure 28.

   Take your stride and start your swing at the ball. You should feel the bottom hand[5] in control since your top hand[30] is in an awkward and weak position.

   As you get closer to the ball you should feel like your top hand can push your bottom hand into the baseball.

   Your bottom hand is still guiding the bat and will hold on past contact because once you make contact with the ball your top hand will have to come off of the handle of the bat because of the awkward grip.

Checkpoints

- You should feel the bottom hand[5] doing most of the work - pulling through keeping a nice bat path through the middle of the field. This drill gives you feel of how much your bottom hand needs to work and when it's time for the top hand[30] to kick in.
- Your top hand[30] is very loosely on the bat, and it's only job is to push.
- As always, hitting line drives is good evidence that you are doing the drill properly. By hitting line drives up the middle using this technique, your hands are getting used to their role in the swing.

15 - Kick Back Drill

Summary

This drill focuses on keeping your front shoulder in[9] when hitting. You can handle more pitches and do a lot of things when you keep your front shoulder from pulling off of the baseball.

This drill also gets your weight shifted in an unorthodox way to your front side. If you have trouble sitting and spinning on your back leg this drill may be helpful. These two issues usually go hand in hand. If your front shoulder opens up too quickly usually you are not properly transferring your weight from your backside[1] to your front side. This drill will tackle both issues.

Purpose

This drill teaches you that even if your base[3] is in a bad position as long as you keep your shoulders closed (square to home plate[24]) as long as possible you still give yourself a chance with your hands. Being able to start your swing with your shoulders square[24] will give the barrel of your bat more coverage through the hitting zone.

As well as staying in line with your shoulders you want to feel that you are transferring your power from your back leg into your front leg. If you spin instead you don't use the power you are creating in your legs properly.

Performing this drill will force you to handle these two issues. If don't get off of your backside[1] or if you are opening up your front shoulder too soon you will either miss the ball or fall over.

Equipment

- Batting Tee

How to Execute this Drill

1.) Set the tee up for a pitch down the middle of the plate. Take your stride as if you were going to hit the baseball.
2.) After a slight pause, start your swing towards the baseball. At the same time take your back leg and kick it back (away from home plate – See Figure 29).

Kicking your back leg away from the plate will force your front side to stay in longer than normal to make up for the awkward feet position. Also, by kicking your leg back you are naturally transferring your weight to your front side. Keep your head looking at the contact point and really focus on keeping your upper half as square to home plate[24] as possible.

Checkpoints

The goal of this drill is to hit line drives up the middle and to the opposite field. By doing this you are over exaggerating the movement you want in the game. This will help keep your front shoulder from opening up too quickly and will help you transfer your weight to your front side properly.

Drill 15
Kick Back Drill
Figure 29

16 - Alternating Fungo and Heavy Bat Drill

Purpose

This isn't for fixing mechanical flaws in a swing like most drills. The combination of using a heavy and light bat will help your overall strength and bat speed.

Why this drill is needed

Think of it this way, you lift weights so you can get stronger. But you need to turn this new strength into functional power for your baseball swing. This concept is why you want to use the heavy and light bat.

Using a heavy bat (depending on how the weight is distributed is about 8-20 ounces heavier than the bat you use for a game) will build overall strength for your hands, forearms, and just for the overall feel of the bat. If you use a heavy bat often your game bat will feel lighter in your hands and it will give you confidence that you will be able to whip the bat[31] through the zone. However, without using a fungo bat in conjunction with your heavy bat training all you will feel is confidence without any extra bat speed.

This drill is meant for bat speed. This is where the fungo bat comes into play. A fungo bat is a specifically designed bat used by coaches for practice. This bat is not meant to hit any sort or pitching, it is not strong enough and will break.

Typical fungo bats are 35-37 inches long and 17-22 ounces. When you put one of these in your hands you will definitely be able to swing it fast. You want your body and fast twitch muscles to feel how quickly you can swing this bat. Sprinters will train by running up hills (strength phase) and running down slight inclines (fast twitch and power phase), this drill takes this same concept and uses it for increased bat speed.

Equipment

1.) Batting Tee
2.) Heavy bat or hitting weights (to add to your normal bat instead of purchasing a heavy bat – See Fig 30)
3.) Fungo bat (i.e. light weight bat)

How to Execute this Drill

1.) Set the tee up for a pitch down the middle of the plate. You can move the tee around but for this drill it isn't necessary.

2.) Start off by using the heavy bat (or add hitting weights to your normal bat) and swing. Be sure to warm up before swinging the heavy bat at full speed. It will be more demanding on your joints, muscles, and hands, so it is highly recommended to begin by swinging a few times at 50% effort.

3.) After you've taken 25 swings with the heavy bat, switch to the fungo bat. Swing full speed about 25 repetitions and get the feel of bat speed. Work on swinging quick, not hard.

Variations of this drill: There are many ways to do the Fungo bat/Heavy bat Drill. You can alternate the bats - swing 10 times then swing the fungo 10 times, then repeat. You can also swing the heavy bat 50 times and then swing the fungo 50 times and be done. Another option is to use the heavy bat one day as a warm up to your normal bat, and on another day, warm up using the fungo bat.

Checkpoints

1.) Don't worry so much about where the ball is going, concentrate on making every swing count.

2.) Remember to work on swinging quick, not hard.

3.) Make sure to not overdo this drill. I would work up to 50 swings with a weighted bat, but not go past that. It can put unneeded pressure on your hands and forearms.

4.) Try this drill a couple times a week and then take notice of how your body feels. This drill can be very valuable when done in moderation.

Figure 30

An alternative to using a heavy bat is to use a bat weight

17 - One Knee Drill

Summary

This drill focuses on two things:

(1) Using your hands and developing your hand/eye coordination, which is critical for all hitters.

(2) Developing a proper bat path. This is a great warm up drill to focus on taking your hands "to" and "through" the baseball. This motion helps keep the barrel in the ideal hitting zone longer.

Purpose

This is a great drill for working on your upper half (everything above your waist) and swing path.

Why does this matter so much? If your swing starts to fall apart, as long as your hands are in a good spot, you still have a chance to make good contact.

When your lower half gets out of sync or it puts you in a weak position, your hands are your last hope for a productive swing. You might get fooled by an off-speed pitch or the ball makes a last second move. When this happens, your arms and hands are your last chance to make adjustments mid-swing.

This is why it is so important to be intimately acquainted your upper body's role in your baseball swing - the feel of the bat in your hands (a feel of where the barrel is at all times) and how to change the speed and direction of the bat as needed.

Isolating your hands and taking your lower half completely out of the drill can help you see how the hands need to work. It will also help you develop your hand/eye coordination. Hand/eye coordination – the ability to put the barrel on the ball - trumps good mechanics every day of the week, and this drill can help you develop that important skill.

Equipment

- Batting Tee

How to Execute this Drill

1. Set up the tee as low as possible.

2. Get on your back knee and straighten your front leg. Check and see that your front foot and back knee are in line with the pitcher.
3. Tee positioning - To start with, set up the tee in line with your front knee (See Figure 31). Move the tee around as desired to practice different types of pitches (If it helps, you can look back at Figure 5).

Keeping correct posture through this drill is VERY IMPORTANT. As you swing, the tendency is to fall backward onto your back knee. Fight against this momentum shift by keeping your weight on the inside part of your back knee as you swing.

At first you may feel like you are fighting to not tip over, but if you keep working on it you will start to feel your balance point. The only way to swing and not fall over is to have a good hand path and swing down through the baseball.

Checkpoints

There are a few things you want to accomplish from this drill.

1.) First, you want to hit a line drive up the middle or a nice one or two hopper to the back of the cage. You don't want any loopy weak line drives or pop ups when doing this drill. Being able to hit a line drive or hard ground ball will show you that you are swinging down on the baseball.

2.) There can be a tendency to want to cheat by collapsing[8] on the back knee and swinging up at the baseball (Figure 32). If you focus on not falling over and hitting line drives, this drill will greatly improve your hands.

Figure 32

18 - STEP BACK DRILL

Summary

The Step Back Drill helps with two things:

(1) Developing a feel for the proper weight shift during the load phase of the baseball swing. Specifically, it will be helpful for those who tend to let their weight get too far over the back foot (see Figure 34). This drill will help you develop a feel for good weight shift.

(2) The Step Back Drill also helps with rhythm. As mentioned earlier, rhythm is a critical part of a good baseball swing. You need to have some easy, tension-free movement before your explosive movement. If you don't, your reaction times and bat speed (i.e. power) will not be optimal. This drill helps you to create rhythm and sync between your base[3] and your hands.

Purpose

A good baseball swing will always have a weight shift phase.

Think of punching someone. For more power, you will draw your fist back before it strikes forward. Another example is a coil or spring, such as a pogo stick. The coil must be compressed before there is any explosive power. You might also think of a snake that coils before it strikes.

The shift of weight to your back leg is how you coil into position of power for the strike. This is a part of rhythm that can store your power in your back leg and use it to explode on the baseball.

If this movement isn't done properly your rhythm and weight shift will be ineffective, causing your power and bat speed to greatly suffer. This drill can help you get this movement right.

This drill is useful to the hitter whose back knee goes beyond their back foot (see Figure 34). Once this happens we lose all of the power that is stored in our legs, putting us in a weak position.

This weak position also interrupts your rhythm, since being too far over your back foot puts you in a poor balance position. You will end up feeling "stuck," which is exactly what rhythm is meant to avoid.

Equipment

- Batting Tee

How to Execute this Drill:

1.) ***Setup*** - Set up the tee for a pitch down the middle of the plate. Address home plate in your normal hitting stance[26]. Next, bring both feet to shoulder width.

2.) ***Rear foot steps back*** - To start this drill take your back foot and put it in the spot you just moved it in from (a couple inches back toward the catcher).

3.) ***Front foot strides forward*** - Next, take your normal stride with your front foot. The action lifting your front creates a weight shift to your back leg.

4.) ***Swing*** – As always, work to hit line drives.

Checkpoints

1.) IMPORTANT – As you shift your weight backward, pay attention to your back knee. Keep it inside of your back foot (see Figure 34). **This is a power position**. Once you get outside your foot and your weight shifts from your big toe to the outside edge of your foot, you have lost this power position.

2.) Checkpoint #2 – Rhythm. Once you can repeat this action with your back knee in the proper position, be sure to keep the rhythm I described in your hands and finish your swing. If it gets choppy, your weight has probably shifted too far toward the catcher. Keeping your back knee inside your back foot (Figure 34) will help maintain rhythm.

3.) Checkpoint #3 - As always, try to hit a line drive back up the middle to the back of the cage.

19 - No Rotation Drill

Summary

With so many moving pieces in a baseball swing, sometimes it's difficult to tell which motion is causing which problem. This drill isolates your upper half so you can work on making it better without the movement of your legs and lower body to interfere.

Purpose

Typically, when the lower half of the body works properly, the rest of the baseball swing follows. The challenge comes when the pitcher manages to mess with your timing or balance.

This is where our plan B comes into play. Even when our base[3] is not perfect, if we have a good idea of how to use our hands we can still hit.

This drill allows you to feel your hands work in your swing. By taking out any lower body action you will notice right away how simple a swing can be. If the lower body action is not perfect it will affect your hands. This drill makes the hands a priority and helps develop a correct hand path without being influenced by other swing variables.

This is a good time to focus on things like the feel of the bat in your hands and where the barrel is, a level bat path, being direct to the baseball, rhythm, having relaxed hands, and other upper body concerns.

This is a good drill to work on developing rhythm. As we've already discussed, the idea of "swing quick not hard" is essential to achieving maximum bat speed. Trying to swing hard causes your body to become tense which causes your big muscles to take over the entire swing and slow your bat speed down. Thinking "quick" allows your body to stay relaxed and function correctly during the swing. The big muscles start the bat then the smaller muscles (forearms, wrists, hands) take over to finish off a whipping action that helps create the best bat speed your body will allow.

Rhythm is a the going to allow you to achieve this goal. It is the slow moving motion that keeps your body relaxed and quick.

Equipment

- Batting Tee

How to Execute this Drill

1.) ***Setup*** - Set up the tee for a pitch down the middle of the plate and address home plate in your normal stance.

2.) ***Feet position*** - Take your normal stride without swinging. In other words, stride like you are about to swing but keep your hands back. Wherever your stride takes you, that is the spot where your feet will stay throughout this entire drill.
3.) ***Weight distribution*** - Get your lower half to a good 50/50 weight distribution between both feet. Once you get into this stance, your legs should stay put. Your back foot will NOT rotate (See Figure 35). This is 100% upper body.
4.) ***Rhythm*** - Have your hands in a comfortable position. Keep them relaxed and moving.
5.) ***Load*** - To get bat speed, you will need to load your hands. They may start in a different place than they would in the game and that's ok.
6.) ***Swing and follow-through*** - Once you make contact with the baseball, keep your feet still. Your follow through will be cut off compared to your normal "long through" follow through. It will be easier to finish with one hand.

Checkpoints:

1.) Focus on keeping rhythm with your relaxed hands as you start your swing. Feel your hands work freely throughout your swing.
2.) Check for a proper, level bat path. Having a level swing often feels more like you are swinging down on the baseball.
3.) Focus on the feel of the bat in your hands, particularly as you move the tee around to simulate different pitches. See how your bat path feels when hitting the pitch inside as compared to the pitch outside, etc.

This simple approach should make it easier to hit every ball on the barrel. It is important to stay relaxed with your upper body and not try to hit the ball too hard. There needs to be a rhythm, a quickness, and relaxed easiness to your swing during this drill. If done properly, this can translate into increased bat speed and more impressive results in games.

20 - Soccer Ball Drill

Summary

The purpose of this drill is to keep all of your weight inside/between your feet. When you get outside of your knees/feet, you will see a significant loss of power. This drill is similar to the Step Back Drill with what it is trying to accomplish, but it does it in a much different way.

This drill will help cut down on head movement. If your head moves during your swing, it keeps you from seeing the ball clearly. If you can't see the ball, you can't hit it.

Another benefit from this drill is that it will not only help you keep your weight on the inside part of your back foot or big toe, it will also help you create power without taking a big stride.

Purpose

This drill helps shorten your stride length, which has several important benefits. Firstly, when you shorten your stride you will naturally cut down your head movement, allowing you to better see the movement and location of the pitch. As I said already, if you can't see the baseball, then you can't hit it. It may sound crazy, but *seeing the baseball* is probably the most overlooked step in hitting – even though it may be one of the most important.

Secondly, if you look at the best hitters in the game, most of them have very small strides. Even those who have leg kicks, their stride foot usually lands only a few inches in front of their initial foot position. A shorter stride makes it easier to stay in a more athletic, powerful position for hitting, and it will eliminate much of the extraneous movement that can easily cause problems – such as causing you to not see the ball or losing your power base.

This drill keeps your weight shift in between your feet. It is common for hitters to get too far back on their back leg so the weight gets outside of their back foot. One way to tell if this is happening to you is to see if your weight is on the outside edge of your foot. This creates balance problems as well as decreased power with your legs. Instead, you want to feel your weight on the inside of your back foot – which is one of the things this drill will help you work on.

Equipment

- Batting Tee
- Soccer Ball, tether ball, basketball, or foursquare ball

How to Execute this Drill

1.) Set up the tee for a pitch down the middle of the plate and address home plate as you would in a game.

2.) Take the soccer ball (tether ball, kick ball, etc.) and place it between your legs above your knees. Keep the ball secure by applying pressure with both legs. This will ensure your weight is distributed correctly, since it is impossible to hold the ball and make the common mistakes we discussed earlier.

3.) With the ball between your legs, grip the bat normally and swing.

Checkpoints

Keep the soccer ball from falling out when you load or stride. If it happens to fall out after you make contact, that's ok.

By applying pressure to the ball between your legs it will be impossible to have your weight too far back in your stance, have too long of a stride and have a lot of head movement. This drill addresses and fixes 3 common problems many hitters deal with.

PART 4 – FINAL THOUGHTS

Bottom of the 9th inning. I hope this book has confirmed for you that the batting tee is not just for young players, but is actually a critical piece of equipment for even the most accomplished big leaguers. Derek Jeter, Troy Tulowitzki, Raul Ibanez… On many occasions I've seen these three All-Stars (and many others) use a batting tee regularly. If these guys use a tee to fine tune and improve their swings, then it's probably a good thing for the rest of us.

The batting tee has been a very important piece of baseball equipment in my career. Preparation is what separates the good from the great players and, as I said before, I've personally observed that even the best players in the world consistently use a tee as one of the two most common daily preparations that ball players use. The other is underhand soft toss.

These drills are the culmination of what other professional players and I are doing on the tee. Sessions off a batting tee are where adjustments start to take place in your swing. It's a much easier progression to make changes off a tee and start implementing them into your soft toss then carrying into batting practice and eventually into the game.

I made reference to a hitting book which was made mandatory reading by the head coach at my junior college, and I am glad it was. *The Mike Schmidt Study* is a great book about the evolution of the baseball swing and what is most useful today. If you want to continue your education on hitting, this book is a must read.

Another book on my recommended reading list, and which fueled my enthusiasm about using a batting tee, is *The Way of Baseball: Finding Stillness at 95 mph*_ by two-time All-Star Shawn Green. He explains how using a batting tee allowed him to slow things down in the batter's box. This book has other facets of course but it primarily talks about how the batting tee allowed him to change his swing and it gave him the confidence to be an incredible big league hitter.

I hope that this book on batting tee drills has been helpful and informative. I strive to give the best information from my experience as well as from other professional players, coaches, and scouts that I have met during my professional playing career. I am available for questions through my website, ProBaseballinsider.com, where you can also find extensive (and free) baseball tips and instruction from the pros.

Play hard!

Doug Bernier

Founder of Probaseballinsider.com

PBI

ProBaseballinsider.com

ABOUT THE AUTHOR: DOUG BERNIER

Doug Bernier, 2012.
Image by Frank Lauri.

Founder of Pro Baseball Insider.com

Doug Bernier debuted in the Major Leagues in 2008 with the Colorado Rockies, and has played professional baseball for 11 years. Most recently, after hitting .361 with the New York Yankees this 2012 spring training where he relieved Derek Jeter at shortstop, Doug spent the 2012 season with the Yankees' triple A team.

Doug founded ProBaseballinsider.com as ***an avenue for pro players, coaches, trainers, and scouts to provide baseball tips and instruction free to the public***. Coaches, parents, and players from beginner to advanced can get in-depth insight into the game of baseball, as well as ask questions and get responses from pro players. These professionals also provide honest insight and critique about what baseball gear is good quality.

If you liked this book and would like more baseball tips and instruction (most of it FREE) check out our website **Pro Baseball Insider.com**, or follow us Twitter **@lowliners** or **Facebook.com/probaseballinsider**

APPENDIX 1 – BASEBALL DEFINITIONS

[1]**Backside -** Is the part of your swing that drives or pushes through the zone. It includes the back foot, back knee, back hip, butt, and back shoulder. All of these parts combine to make the backside of your swing.

[2]**Backspin -** When a ball has front to back spin. This spin will make the ball travel straighter and further. Similar spin to a pitchers fastball.

[3]**Base** – Is used interchangeably with "**bottom half". Everything beneath your waist: Both feet, both knees, both legs and hips.

[4]**Bottom half** – Is used interchangeably in this book with the term "base"**.** Is everything beneath your waist: Both feet, both knees, both legs, and hips. This is sometimes referred to as "lower half".

[5]**Bottom Hand** – This is the hand of your lead arm. It is also the closest hand to the knob of the bat. For a right-handed hitter, the bottom hand is his left hand; and for a lefty the bottom hand would be his right hand.

[6]**Cast barrel -** Also "casting your barrel;" Is when the barrel of your bat gets away from your body too quickly or enters the hitting zone too soon. The goal is to keep the barrel inside the baseball[11] as long as possible, if the barrel gets outside the baseball you are casting your barrel. This will slow your bat speed down considerably and you will see a lot of weak ground balls to the pull side.

[7]**Center line** – The center line is an ideal imaginary axis line which is drawn through the hitter's body during the baseball swing *at the point of contact*. The line should be drawn through the hitter's head, body and back knee, ending at the ground at the midpoint between your feet.

[8]**Collapsing backside -** This term describes what happens if any part of your back side (Back foot, back knee, back hip, butt, and back shoulder) fails to stay strong, tall and level. If one of these parts doesn't stay level, it will cause the batter to have an uppercut swing. If the shoulders remain level and the swing is level that is a good indicator that your backside is strong and is not collapsing.

[9]**Front shoulder in** or **Front shoulder closed -** This is keeping your front shoulder as still as possible as you start your swing. Hitters that over swing tend to assist their legs by pulling with their front shoulder, opening up their body too early making them susceptible to pitches on the outer half of the plate.

A good key is to start with your chin on your front shoulder and keep it there until you know the location of the pitch and start to swing (also see Drill #15 – the Kick Back Drill).

[10]**Groove the swing -** Is another way of saying a hitter can successfully repeat his swing in games as well as in practice. As former MLB All-Star Albie Pearson explained in his introduction, "it takes time and many thousands of swings to craft an effective baseball swing, and to make that swing so second-nature that your body will react with good mechanics when you face live pitching and split-second timing in a game." When you can regularly take your "A" swing into the games, you have successfully grooved your swing.

[11]**Inside the Ball** – This term can be used in either of the following two ways:

(1) to describe the place on the baseball where you ideally want to make contact. If you took a vertical axis and stuck it through a baseball, the half of the ball closest to you is the inside part of the ball. Hitting this area on a baseball gives you the best probability of hitting line drives and driving balls with the proper backspin; and

(2) "Inside the baseball" can also be used to describe the area between the baseball and your body. In a mechanically sound baseball swing, you want to keep your bat and hands inside the baseball. This means keep your hands and the entire bat in the space between the ball and your body as long as possible. This is the ideal path to the baseball, and it is the opposite of the term "casting your barrel."

[12]**Elbow in the slot** – This is when your back elbow is tucked tightly into the side of your body. This is an important part of your swing for several reasons. It helps you keep your hands inside the baseball and it keeps the barrel of the bat on the proper bat path. If your elbow is "in the slot", then it will keep your barrel above your hands until it reaches the hitting zone and then allows the barrel to level out as it goes through the zone. This is a better bat path to make contact with the baseball consistently and avoid the dreaded "swing and miss."

[13]**Flat Bat** - This refers to when the bat is going through the hitting zone and your hands and the barrel of the bat are level. This should happen just before contact, at contact, and just after contact.

Note: Sometimes people use this to refer to your set up and holding your bat so its parallel to the ground.

[14]**Jammed** – From time to time, you may hear the common baseball phrase "getting jammed." This happens when the baseball makes contact with the bat too close to the batter's hands, or in other words, somewhere between the ideal contact on the barrel and the batter's hands. It usually happens on a sinker or fastball in, or if the baseball swing was a little late. Often the result is a broken bat or vibrating stinging hands.

[15]**Launch position** – This is your body position after load and separation[20]; it is the moment you begin to fire your bat at the baseball. While separation[20] is getting into a strong position to hit, the launch position is the point where you start your swing. Your front foot is down, hands are back somewhere between your back shoulder and ear height.

[16]**Linear movement – This term should NOT be confused with the Linear Method of Hitting.** The word "linear" means in a line (as opposed to spinning or rotating), but this should not be confused with the Linear Method of Hitting, which takes the concept of linear motion to its extreme. It should be noted that even highly rotational swings often have some elements of linear movement in them. This book reflects the idea that the best baseball players use a combination of linear and rotational motion in their baseball swings.

In baseball, linear movement simply means moving toward or transferring the weight from your backside to your front side.

Linear movement is done with a firm front leg so your body can stay behind your front foot. <u>This is done with your bottom half[4] so your head can stay still and see the ball clearly</u>. Linear movement in a baseball swing is beneficial for several reasons: (1) It keeps the bat in the hitting zone longer and increases your chances of making solid contact with the baseball; (2) Keeps your body motion and bat path driving through the baseball instead of pulling off toward third base (or toward 1st base if you are left handed hitter).

[17]**Losing the barrel -** Is when the barrel of your bat dips below your hands. You want the barrel of the bat above your hands as long as possible until it levels out just before the point of contact. This is easier to see from a side view (ex. 1st base side when watching a right handed hitter). Losing the barrel creates extra length in your swing making it slower and less efficient.

[18]**Palm up / Palm down -** Is the strongest position you can be in with your hands and bat **at the point of contact**.

If you were to open your top hand[30] at contact it should be facing up. If you were to open up your bottom hand at contact it should be facing down towards the ground.

A common problem happens when hitters lose this power position because they roll the wrist over too early in the swing process.

[19]**Rolling over the wrist too early** - A common problem happens when hitters lose this power position because they roll the wrist over too early in the swing process. The ideal and most powerful hitting form is to be in the palm up/palm down[18] position at contact.

[20]**Separation -** Is a power position achieved when your front foot strides away from your hands and makes contact with the ground. When done correctly you will feel a tightness in your front side (oblique area). This position resembles a stretched rubber band before its let go. This stretching of your body produces bat speed and power. Separation is getting into a strong position to hit.

[21]**Short to the ball** - See **shortening your swing.** Being "short to the ball" is quickening or shortening the distance that your bat has to travel from the time you decide to swing up to contact.

[22]**Shortening your swing -** Is taking out unnecessary movement in your swing up until the contact point. This never ending project allows you to wait longer to swing. The goal is to make every move count in your swing from the setup to contact.

[23]**Space** – In this book, space refers to distance necessary for the bat to build up speed and make contact with the baseball in the optimal hitting zone/angle. The phrase "create space" or "creating space" refers to the bad habits a hitter can fall into when his timing is off and the ball gets too deep into the hitting zone.

When this happens, the natural tendency is to fall back onto our back leg to create more room to hit the ball without getting jammed[14]. These actions usually do more harm than good. If you are late with your swing and feel like the pitch is beating you, you should still hit through the ball even if it means you may get jammed.

[24]**Square to home plate** - This is when your feet and shoulders are in a straight line towards the pitcher. Your stance[26] is neither open nor closed. Your body, belt buckle, and knees are facing home plate. Also referred to as "square stance[27]".

[25]**Squash the bug** - This term has been used to teach hitters to rotate on their back foot. Rotation is good but when you spin on the ball of your back foot there is a negative tendency for your swing to produce an uppercut. Your bat will be in and out of the hitting zone too quickly. Instead of rotating on the ball of your foot, think of rotating by getting your back foot on its toe. This will help flatten and keep your bat in the zone longer which is ideal.

[26]**Stance – also "batting stance" or "hitting stance."** This refers to your body position and feet placement when you are ready to hit and before your baseball swing begins.

Commonly used terms include "open," "closed," and "square[24]". An open stance is when your front foot in your hitting stance is further away from home plate then your back foot. Alternatively, closed refers to when your front foot is closer to home plate than your back foot.

A stance may also be referred to as narrow or wide, which refers to the distance between your feet. Naturally, a wide stance will be a lower one.

[27]**Tight** - Is the term used to describe your hands staying close to your body as you deliver the barrel of the bat to the baseball. Your hands will stay close to your body right up until contact where you will throw your hands in the direction of the ball.

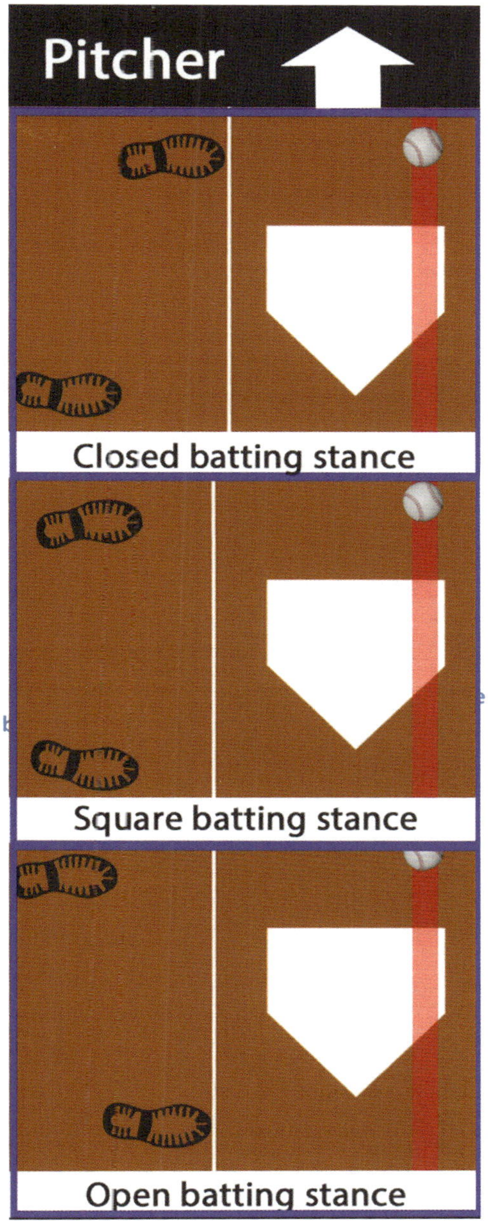

[28]**Tightening up** - See **Tight.** It's not the opposite of staying loose and relaxed with your swing. This refers to eliminating unnecessary movement from your swing, keeping your hands close to your body as you bring the bat to contact. This is also known as making your swing more efficient.

[29]**Topspin** - When a ball has a back to front spin. This spin makes the ball fall to the ground quicker and it doesn't travel as far. Similar spin to a pitchers curve ball.

[30]**Top Hand** – May also be called the rear arm. When you grip a bat its the closes hand toward the trademark. A right handed hitter's top hand would be his right hand. A lefty's top hand would be his left hand.

[31]**Whip the bat** - Is a term meaning quick bat speed. Don't swing hard - this uses big muscles, slowing your swing down. Instead, swing quick. This lets your big muscles start your swing but you will finish with your hands, quickening your swing.

APPENDIX 2 – ANATOMY OF A BASEBALL BAT

Anatomy of the baseball bat - This chart clarifies terminology relating to the baseball bat.

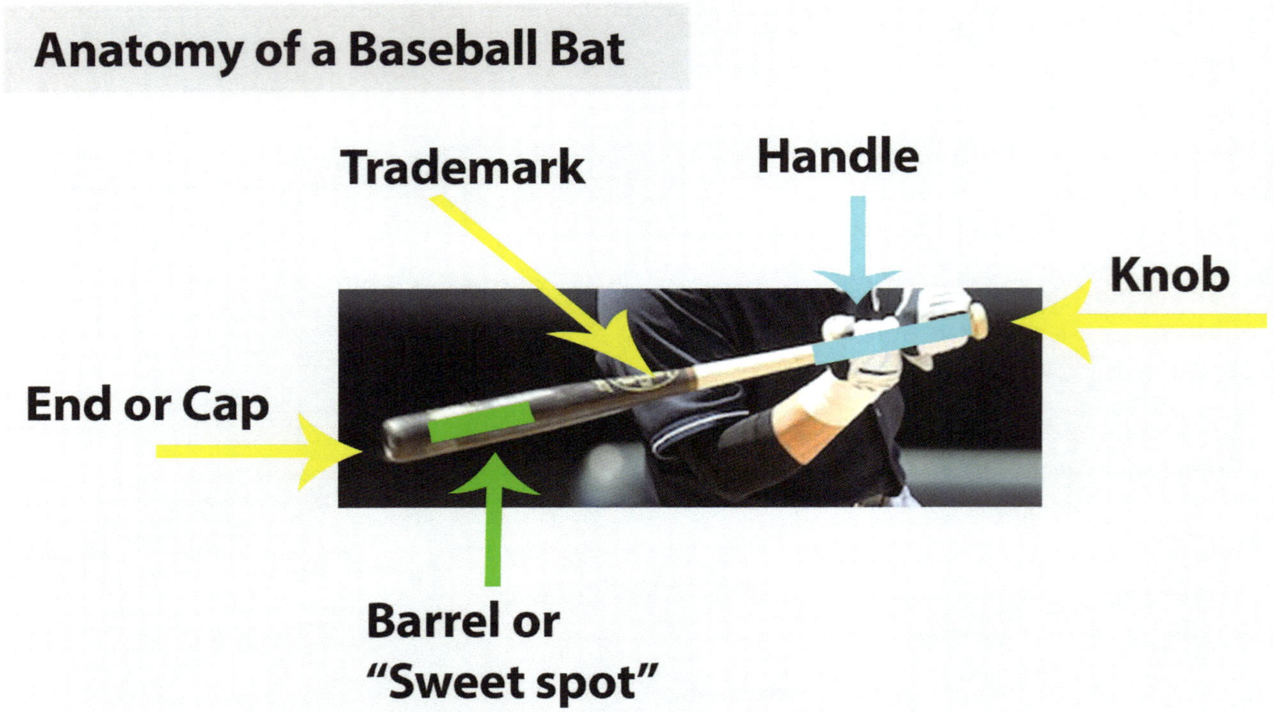

BIBLIOGRAPHY

Schmidt, M. & Ellis, R. (1994). *The Mike Schmidt Study: Hitting theory, skills and technique.* Atlanta: McGriff & Bell.

Yellin, S. & Biancalana, B. (2010). *7 Secrets of World Class Athletes*. Createspace Independent Publishing.

DISCLAIMER

THE INFORMATION IN THIS BOOK IS MEANT TO SUPPLEMENT, NOT REPLACE, PROPER BASEBALL TRAINING. LIKE ANY SPORT INVOLVING SPEED, EQUIPMENT, BALANCE AND ENVIRONMENTAL FACTORS, BASEBALL POSES SOME INHERENT RISK. READERS ARE ADVISED TO TAKE FULL RESPONSIBILITY FOR THEIR SAFETY AND KNOW THEIR LIMITS. BEFORE PRACTICING THE SKILLS DESCRIBED IN THIS BOOK, BE SURE THAT YOUR EQUIPMENT IS WELL MAINTAINED, AND DO NOT TAKE RISKS BEYOND YOUR LEVEL OF EXPERIENCE, APTITUDE, TRAINING, AND COMFORT LEVEL. THE AUTHOR, PUBLISHER AND EDITORS OF THIS BOOK ASSUME NO LIABILITY FOR ACTIONS TAKEN ACCORDING TO THE ADVICE OF THIS BOOK, AND THE ACTIONS DESCRIBED IN THIS BOOK ARE PERFORMED AT THE READER'S OWN RISK.

33423802R00038

Made in the USA
Lexington, KY
24 June 2014